EYEWITNESS EXP

BUG
HUNTER

by David Burnie

Consultants Nathan Erwin and Dr. Gary Hevel, National
Museum of Natural History, Smithsonian Institution

SMITHSONIAN

Penguin
Random
House

For Bookwork Ltd:
Editors Louise Pritchard, Annabel Blackledge
Art Editors Jill Plank, Kate Mullins

For Dorling Kindersley Ltd
Senior Editors Fran Baines, Carey Scott
Senior Art Editor Stefan Podhorodecki
Managing Editor Linda Esposito
Managing Art Editor Jane Thomas
Jacket Designer Chris Drew
Jacket Copywriter/Editor Adam Powley, Carrie Love
Publishing Managers Caroline Buckingham, Andrew Macintyre
Art Director Simon Webb
Publishing Director Jonathan Metcalf
Production Controller Erica Rosen
Picture Researcher Sarah Pownall
DK Picture Library Sarah Mills
DTP Designer Natasha Lu
Photography Dave King

REVISED EDITION
Project Art Editor Deep Shikha Walia
Editor Suneha Dutta
Art Editors Mary Sandberg, Shipra Jain, Shreya Sadhan
Senior Editors Carron Brown, Shatarupa Chaudhuri
DTP Designer Bimlesh Tiwary
Senior DTP Designer Harish Aggarwal
Managing Editors Linda Esposito, Alka Thakur Hazarika
Managing Art Editors Michael Duffy, Romi Chakraborty
CTS Manager Balwant Singh
Publisher Andrew Macintyre
Producer, Pre-production Lucy Sims
Senior Producer Gemma Sharpe
Jacket Editors Claire Gell, Maud Whatley
Jacket Designers Laura Brim, Dhirendra Singh
Managing Jacket Editor Saloni Singh
Jacket Development Manager Sophia MTT
Publishing Director Jonathan Metcalf
Associate Publishing Director Liz Wheeler
Art Director Phil Ormerod

SMITHSONIAN ENTERPRISES
Product Development Manager Kealy Wilson
Licensing Manager Ellen Nanney
Vice President, Education and Consumer Products Brigid Ferraro
**Senior Vice President, Education
and Consumer Products** Carol LeBlanc
President Chris Liedel

First American Edition, 2005
This American Edition, 2015
Published in the United States by
DK Publishing, 345 Hudson Street
New York, New York 10014

Copyright © 2005, © 2015 Dorling Kindersley Limited
A Penguin Random House Company
2 4 6 8 10 9 7 5 3 1
001–SD133–Jan/2015

A catalog record for this book is available
from the Library of Congress.
ISBN 978-1-4654-3016-8

DK books are available at special discounts when purchased in bulk
for sales promotions, premiums, fund-raising, or educational use.
For details, contact: DK Publishing Special Markets, 345 Hudson Street,
New York, New York 10014
SpecialSales@dk.com

Color reproduction by Alta Image Ltd, London, UK
Printed in China

A WORLD OF IDEAS:
SEE ALL THERE IS TO KNOW

Contents

The world of bugs

Whether you live in the country or in a city, bugs are never far away. Most of them live outdoors, although, given the chance, quite a few will flutter, hop, or scuttle into people's homes. But what exactly is a bug? Why are they such successful animals? And what is the difference between bugs and other creepy-crawlies? To find out the answers to all these questions, the place to start is right here!

The legs and wings are attached to the insect's middle part, or thorax

An insect's body is covered by a hard skeleton, which works like a case

Bug basics

Real bugs are always insects. There are more than a million different kinds of insects, which makes them the most numerous animals on Earth. Unlike other creepy-crawlies, insects' bodies are divided into three parts—head, thorax, and abdomen. They have six legs, and most insects have wings. For insects, being able to fly is a huge plus. It is one of the reasons they are so widespread.

STUDYING INSECTS

Scientists who study insects are called entomologists. They work all over the world, identifying new species and investigating the way insects live. Some entomologists study farmland insects, particularly those that pollinate plants or feed on crops. Medical entomologists study insects that spread diseases as they feed.

◀ **Bug research**
This entomologist is investigating insects from the tropical forests of Costa Rica. Every year, entomologists identify thousands of new insects from all over the world, but lots more are still waiting to be discovered.

Insects have a pair of antennae, or feelers, on their heads

This beetle's abdomen is covered by its wings and thorax

This ladybug is in proportion to the huge beetle above

Ladybug

Identity parade

Lots of animals look like insects, but are built in different ways. Crustaceans have lots of legs, spiders always have eight, and centipedes and millipedes can have hundreds. Of all these animals, insects are the only ones with wings.

Crustacean

Spider

Centipede

Millipede

Insect

Lice use their claws to cling to hairs

Eeeeeek!

Why is it that bugs give so many people the creeps? Sometimes it is because they can bite or sting, and sometimes it has to do with the unpredictable way they move. Some bugs scuttle around in a jerky way, while others land on our clothes or skin. Some even live aboard people—this louse is clinging to a human hair.

Essential equipment

Because insects are small, you need to get close to see how they work. One way to do this is to collect them—see below to find out what to pack in your collecting kit. To get a good look at most bugs, you will need a magnifying glass or hand lens. A magnifying glass enlarges by about two or three times, which is enough to see lots of extra detail. A hand lens is even better because it magnifies by about ten times, but is small enough to fit in a pocket.

BUG HUNTER'S CODE

When you go bug-hunting, it is important that you do not harm any bugs or yourself. Stick to these three rules:
- Don't touch any bug with your bare hands unless you know that it is harmless.
- If you collect a bug to study it, release it when you have finished.
- If you go bug-hunting at night, make sure you have an adult with you.

COLLECTING KIT

The most important part of a bug-collecting kit is a set of containers for living animals. Jelly jars are good, if you make air holes in their lids. You can also use empty margarine tubs, as long as you wash and rinse them thoroughly. Use a thumbtack to make air holes in the lid, put in some paper towels as padding, and your bug box is ready.

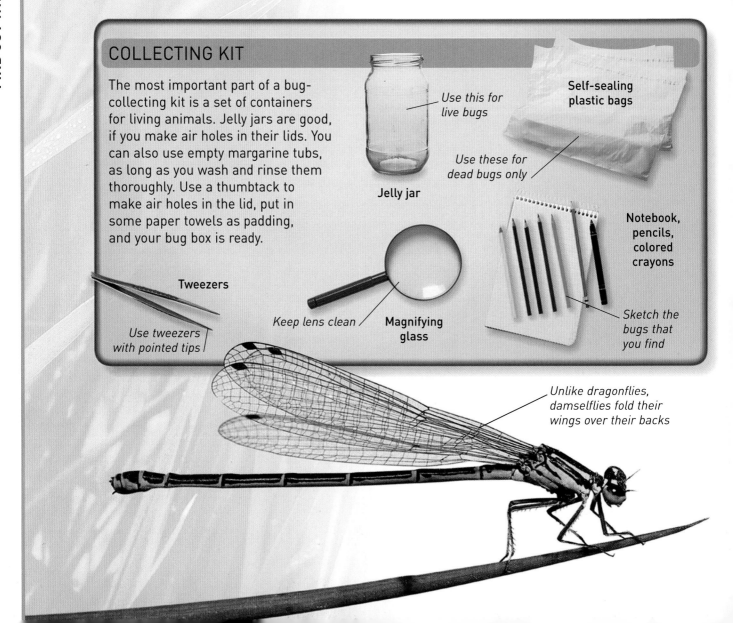

Use this for live bugs

Self-sealing plastic bags

Use these for dead bugs only

Jelly jar

Notebook, pencils, colored crayons

Tweezers

Use tweezers with pointed tips

Keep lens clean

Magnifying glass

Sketch the bugs that you find

Unlike dragonflies, damselflies fold their wings over their backs

IDENTIFYING BUGS

When looking at bugs, run through the list of features below, and then check the field-guide flaps. You'll soon be able to tell one type of insect from another.

- Long, slender body and four wings that stick out sideways: dragonfly
- Long, slender body and four wings that fold back: damselfly
- Long body and extra-large back legs, with, or sometimes without, wings: cricket or grasshopper
- Broad body and mouthparts that pierce and suck: plant bug

- Hardened forewings that fit over abdomen like a case: beetle
- Two-winged flying insect: true fly
- Big, colourful wings held above body at rest: butterfly
- Narrow waist, slender wings, and bright stripes: bee or wasp

Hardened forewings

Beetle

Soft brush for nudging bugs

Magnifying glass clearly shows the dragonfly's eyes

Wing veins vary between different types of dragonflies

Using a magnifying glass

Hold the magnifying glass close to the insect, then gradually pull it away until the insect is in focus. Use a soft cloth to keep the lens clean.

A dragonfly's color helps to identify it

Bug habitats

When you start bug-watching, you'll soon notice that different bugs live in different places. For example, bees and butterflies stay close to flowers, while dragonflies prefer ponds and streams. Woodlice live in leaf litter— a layer of dead leaves under shrubs and trees. These different places are called habitats. A habitat is more than just a home. It gives a bug everything it needs to survive, including food and the right conditions for breeding.

Freshwater ▶

Lots of bugs live in freshwater, so ponds are good places for bug-watching. Some insects live on the surface, while others swim below it. Dragonflies speed through the air, catching other insects on the wing. If you have a dip net, you'll find that swimming bugs are easy to catch. Be careful not to touch them because some of them can bite!

◀ Leaf litter

One of the best places to hunt bugs is in leaf litter—the layer of leaves under trees and shrubs that extends down to the crumbly compost that forms when dead leaves rot down. Leaf litter is home to many kinds of insects, and other creepy-crawlies as well. Many leaf litter animals, such as this woodlouse, like surroundings that are dark and damp.

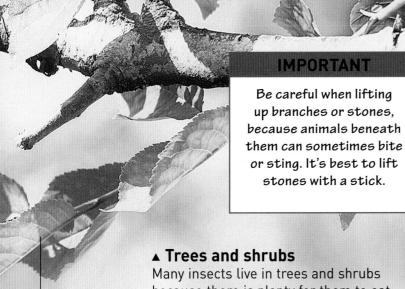

▲ Trees and shrubs

Many insects live in trees and shrubs because there is plenty for them to eat. Caterpillars and crickets feed on leaves, while aphids suck up sap. Look for leaves that have been chewed on by beetles and caterpillars. Many of these insects are well camouflaged because they need to hide from birds.

Leaves are ideal places for bugs to hide

◄ Grass and flowers

Flowery places are perfect for spotting butterflies, bees, and hoverflies. These insects visit flowers to feed on nectar—a sugary liquid food. Sunny days are best because nectar-feeders like to be warm as they work.

WHERE TO LOOK

- Dragonflies and damselflies—ponds
- Woodlice, centipedes, and millipedes—leaf litter and under trees
- Moth caterpillars and sap-sucking bugs— trees and shrubs
- Butterflies, bees, and hoverflies—gardens and flowery grassland
- Beetles—on the ground and in leaf litter
- Spiders—grassy places and under stones

▲ Walls and paving

In warm weather, walls and paving are good places to spot mini-animals on the move. Wall wildlife includes tiny red velvet mites, and jumping spiders, which leap onto their prey.

Bugs indoors

You don't have to go outside to see bugs, because some kinds live indoors. Indoor bugs include temporary visitors, such as flies and mosquitoes, and long-term residents, such as spiders. Spiders are useful animals to have indoors, because they keep insects under control.

Kitchens

In summer, houseflies and bluebottles often fly into kitchens through open doors and windows. They come indoors to look for food or for somewhere to lay their eggs.

Houseflies are often found in kitchens

Basements and bathrooms

Spiders often lurk in quiet corners in basements or attics, but some wander around after dark. House spiders can get trapped in bathtubs because they cannot climb the slippery sides.

House spiders use their legs to feel their way

Drawers and cupboards

Silverfish live in cupboards, where they eat tiny specks of spilled food. Clothes moths sometimes live in drawers and closets—their tiny caterpillars feed on wool.

Silverfish eat starchy and sweet food, including flour and sugar

Hide and seek

Insects are all around us, but many are so well camouflaged that they are hard to spot. However, with the help of a tray and a piece of white paper, you can bring them out into the open. Most camouflaged insects live on plants, so shrubs and trees are good places to start. Tap a branch with a stick, and insects will tumble on to the tray. They will be easy to see on the white paper.

WHAT YOU WILL NEED

- Shallow tray
- White paper
- Scissors
- Stick
- Magnifying glass

Always ask an adult for help when using sharp scissors.

IMPORTANT

Don't pick up any of the bugs you collect because they may bite or sting. Let them crawl or fly back to where they came from.

1 **Cut a piece** of white paper to fit the bottom of your tray. Line the tray with the paper.

2 **Place the tray** under a leafy branch. Then gently tap the branch with a stick—or ask a friend to do it so you can see the insects tumble out.

INSECT CAMOUFLAGE

In the insect world, camouflage works in two ways. Many bugs use it to hide from their enemies, such as lizards and sharp-eyed birds. Predatory bugs are also camouflaged, so they can stalk or ambush their prey. Camouflage works best when a bug keeps perfectly still. Unlike humans, insects are very good at this. They can stay in the same position for hours without feeling uncomfortable or bored.

Living twig ▶
This peppered moth caterpillar hides from its enemies by looking like a twig. Its skin is the same color as bark. Its head is short and flat, making it look as if the top of the "twig" has snapped off.

GIFTED MIMICS

Insects aren't always quite what they seem. Some harmless kinds look like ones that sting, and they even move like them. These insect mimics fool many people, but if you know your bugs, you will be able to see through their disguise. Next time you see a bee or a wasp, look carefully to see if it is the real thing or a fake.

Wasp-mimicking flies ▼
Hoverflies often mimic wasps. Unlike real wasps, they have two wings instead of four, and they do not have a stinger.

Hoverfly

Wasp

Shield bugs and their young rely on camouflage to survive

3 **Use the magnifying glass** to get a close-up view of the insects as they fly or crawl away. Try using the tray under different plants to see which bugs live where.

Tricks and traps

The world is a dangerous place for insects because they are a food source. Fortunately, insects have many ways of hiding and of fighting back. Wherever you are, it's easy to spot insects that survive thanks to some clever tricks and traps. Some of the most common insect tricksters are click beetles and small sap-suckers called spittlebugs. Spittlebugs blow bubbles to make a sticky froth to hide in. If you see a frothy mass on a plant, wipe the foam away with a finger. You will find a soft-bodied bug inside.

Hiding in foam

Spittlebugs suck sap from grasses and other soft-stemmed plants. Adult spittlebugs can quickly hop away from danger, but young ones can only crawl. A shield of frothy bubbles helps to keep them out of harm's way. The best time to look for spittlebug froth is in spring and early summer.

WHERE TO LOOK

- Spittlebugs—on plants in gardens and grassy places
- Ant lions—on the ground in warm places with loose, sandy soil
- Click beetles—on plants in gardens, grassy places, and fields
- Bombardier beetles— on the ground among stones or fallen leaves

This young spittlebug has been revealed by wiping away its froth

Spittlebug froth is sometimes known as cuckoo spit, although it is not made by birds

Insect artillery

Ant lion grubs dig pits in sandy soil and then lurk inside them. If another insect walks by, the ant lion flicks sand at it to make it fall into the pit. If you find an ant lion pit, try tapping a blade of grass on the edge. The ant lion will flick sand at it, mistaking it for prey.

Ant lion grubs have camouflaged bodies and extra-large jaws for gripping their prey

Playing dead

If you find a click beetle, try putting it in the palm of your hand. At first, the beetle will pretend to be dead. A few seconds later, it will click a hinge behind its head, which throws it into the air. Click beetles use this trick to escape from their enemies.

When it pretends to be dead, a click beetle folds up its legs against its body

CHEMICAL WEAPONRY

The bombardier beetle is a famous expert in self-defense. If it feels threatened by another animal, it releases poisonous chemicals into a chamber inside its abdomen. The chemicals explode, spraying a jet of hot gas out of its body and toward its attacker. The beetle can produce up to 50 explosions in a row, giving it a chance to run away.

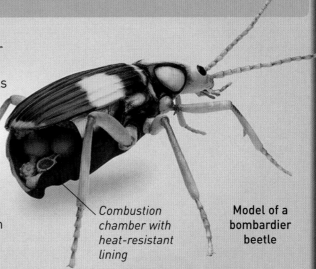

Explosive defense ▶
The bombardier beetle has a special combustion chamber for mixing poisonous chemicals. It can swivel the tip of its abdomen to aim the spray.

Combustion chamber with heat-resistant lining

Model of a bombardier beetle

Insects in the air

In spring and summer, the air is often filled with flying insects. To get a close look at them, try making this butterfly net. Trawl your net just above flowers or tall grass, and you will be amazed how many flying insects you catch. To examine your haul, hold the handle out straight and let the net hang down. The insects inside will gradually crawl out and fly away.

WHAT YOU WILL NEED

- 32-x-32-in (80-x-80-cm) square of muslin
- Stapler and staples
- Wire coat hanger
- Pliers
- 24-in (60-cm) stick
- 4-in (10-cm) flexible wire
- Strong adhesive tape

Ask an adult to help you with the coat hanger.

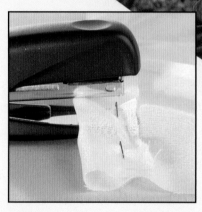

1 **Fold over** about 2¼ in (6 cm) along one edge of the cloth. Staple it down all the way along to make a hem.

HANDY TIP

Your net will be easier to swing to and fro if the handle is no more than 24 in (60 cm) long.

2 **Use the pliers** to straighten the hanger. Slide it through the hem, then grip the hanger by both ends, and carefully bend it to form a circle. Straighten the ends of the hanger so that they are ready to be taped to the stick.

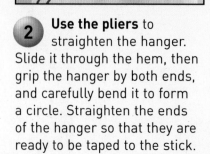

3 **Put the stick** across the mouth of the net, and use the flexible wire to tie the stick to the far side. Then fasten the straight ends of the hanger to the stick using the tape.

INSECT WINGS

Compared to birds, insects have very varied wings. If you look carefully at a fly, you will see that it has just two wings, but most other insects have four. Sometimes, the front and back wings look the same, but often they are different. Beetles have extra-tough front wings, called elytra, which fit over their hind wings like a case. This case protects beetles' delicate hind wings from injury as they crawl around.

▲ **Lacewing**
A lacewing has four wings, and each one is crisscrossed by a network of veins. These strengthen the wings, and keep them in shape while they beat up and down.

TAKING OFF

▲ **Up and away**
A ladybug has to open its spotted front wings, then unpack its hind wings, which are folded underneath.

Flies can take off almost instantly, which is why they are so hard to swat. But for some insects—such as beetles—getting airborne takes a bit of preparation. Ladybugs need several seconds to get their wings ready, so instead of flying away they often prefer to walk. If you find a ladybug on a plant and nudge it with a blade of grass, you may see it open its wings and, after a moment, fly away.

4 Finally, use the **stapler** to stitch together the side and bottom of the net. Your net is now ready to use.

After dark

Lots of bugs are on the move after dark, when humans are asleep. Some bugs fly through the night air, but many more crawl and scuttle over the ground. By making a simple pitfall trap, it is easy to catch these nocturnal creepy-crawlies. Then you can return to the trap during the day to examine your catch.

WHAT YOU WILL NEED

- Trowel
- Plastic cup or glass jar
- Food for baiting (cheese, fruit, or meat)
- Four small stones, corks, or marbles
- Tile or plywood about 4 in (10 cm) square
- Magnifying glass

IMPORTANT

Don't go outside after dark without an adult, and remember to release the insects you catch when you are finished studying them.

1 **Dig a hole** in soft ground and bury the cup or jar exactly up to its rim. Place a piece of bait inside the cup or jar.

2 **Put the stones** on the ground around the cup or jar, and place the tile over the top to make a rainproof roof.

3 **Leave the trap** overnight and examine your catch in the morning. You can dig up the jar and take it indoors for a closer look. Vary the bait to see if it attracts different bugs.

BEETLES ON THE PROWL

Night patrol ▲
Ground beetles hunt caterpillars and other garden pests.

Many beetles are nocturnal hunters that feed on the ground. They are ideally built for this kind of life, with sturdy legs and hard front wings that fit over their back like a case to protect their delicate hind wings. Ground beetles are often black. This camouflages them in the darkness, providing some protection from predators.

LIGHTING UP

Unlike most nocturnal insects, fireflies and glowworms are easy to find because they light up after dark. These insects make light inside their bodies and use it to attract a mate. Glowworms light up on the ground, but fireflies light up on trees or bushes, or while they are flying. If you disturb one of these insects, its light will often dim or go out. But if you stay nearby and keep still, it will slowly come back on.

◀ Glowing in the dark

This female glowworm is signaling to males flying overhead. Her light comes from special organs underneath her abdomen. Unlike the males, the female does not have wings and cannot fly.

Attracted by the smell of food, beetles and other animals fall into the trap and cannot climb back out

Butterfly bar

With their bright colors, butterflies are many people's favorite insects. Like moths, they feed at flowers, sucking up sugary nectar with their tongues. To get a close look at butterflies feeding, make a butterfly bar. Instead of nectar, the bar serves a sticky mixture of sugar and overripe fruit—something most butterflies cannot resist. After dark, try leaving the bar open to attract hungry moths.

WHAT YOU WILL NEED

- Overripe banana
- Mixing bowl
- Fork
- Saucepan
- Wooden spoon
- 1/2 cup unrefined dark brown sugar
- 1 cup water
- Paper plate
- Pencil
- String

Ask an adult to help with cooking.

1 **Peel the banana**, slice it, and put the slices in the bowl. Use the fork to mash it into a paste.

2 **Mix the banana** paste, sugar, and water in the saucepan. Heat the mixture until it simmers, then leave it cooking until it becomes sticky. Turn off the heat and let it cool.

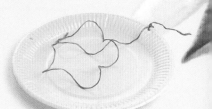

3 **Make three holes** in the plate with the pencil. Tie a piece of string around the plate through each hole.

BUTTERFLY OR MOTH?

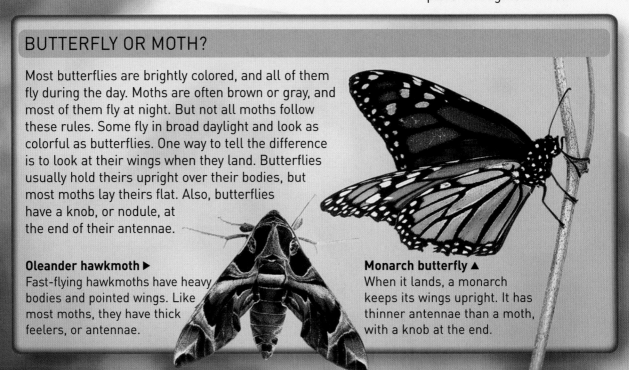

Most butterflies are brightly colored, and all of them fly during the day. Moths are often brown or gray, and most of them fly at night. But not all moths follow these rules. Some fly in broad daylight and look as colorful as butterflies. One way to tell the difference is to look at their wings when they land. Butterflies usually hold theirs upright over their bodies, but most moths lay theirs flat. Also, butterflies have a knob, or nodule, at the end of their antennae.

Oleander hawkmoth ▶
Fast-flying hawkmoths have heavy bodies and pointed wings. Like most moths, they have thick feelers, or antennae.

Monarch butterfly ▲
When it lands, a monarch keeps its wings upright. It has thinner antennae than a moth, with a knob at the end.

ROLL-UP TONGUES

If you watch butterflies feeding, you will see that their tongues work like drinking straws. A butterfly tests the food with its tongue and then starts to feed. When it has finished feeding, it coils up its tongue beneath its head. This means the tongue is out of harm's way when the butterfly takes to the air.

▲ **Getting ready**
This butterfly is unrolling its tongue so that it can start to feed.

Butterflies can sense sweet food with their antennae and with their feet

The mixture should be slightly runny so butterflies can suck it up

4 **Tie the plate** to a low branch, then smear on the paste. Stand back and watch the butterflies arrive.

WHAT YOU WILL NEED

- 1 1/2-gal (5-liter) plastic bottle
- Scissors
- Piece of muslin
- Jelly jar
- Water
- Food plants
- Caterpillars
- Large, thick elastic band

Raising caterpillars

If you are an avid bug-watcher, it's hard to beat the excitement of seeing caterpillars turn into adult butterflies. It's not difficult to find caterpillars, but if you want to keep them, you need to make a suitable home for them. One of the best ways is to use a large plastic bottle fitted with a fabric roof. This lets the caterpillars get the fresh air that they need.

1 **Cut off** the sloping sides and top of the bottle. Cut out a square of muslin around the bottom of the bottle, about 2 in (5 cm) bigger all round.

2 **Fill the jelly jar** with water and stand the caterpillar food plants in the water. Put the jar and plants in the bottle.

3 **Carefully put** the caterpillars on the plants. Then put the muslin over the top of the bottle and use the elastic band to hold it in place.

SHEDDING SKIN

In order to grow, all bugs have to shed their skeleton—which looks like skin—every so often. Each time they do this, they leave the old, empty skeleton behind. Caterpillars usually drop them on the ground, but spiders often leave theirs hanging from their webs. People often mistake the empty skeletons for living spiders, but it's easy to find out which is which. Touch it gently with a pencil—a skeleton won't scuttle away!

A fresh start ▲
This spider has just finished shedding its skeleton. Its old skeleton is above it, held in place by strands of silk. Spiders shed their skeletons many times in their lives. Insects stop once they have become adults.

IMPORTANT

Caterpillars are picky eaters, so give yours the same plants that you found them on. Remember to check the water level in the jelly jar every day, so the leaves do not wilt.

Changing shape

All insects change shape as they grow up. Grasshoppers change gradually each time they shed their skins. Young grasshoppers look like their parents, but without wings. Butterflies and moths change in a different way. They start life as caterpillars and change totally during a resting stage called a pupa.

◄ Egg
Most insects hatch from eggs. Butterflies glue their eggs to the leaves of plants so the caterpillars have food.

Caterpillar ▶
A caterpillar's job is to eat. As the caterpillar feeds, it grows quickly and sheds its skeleton several times.

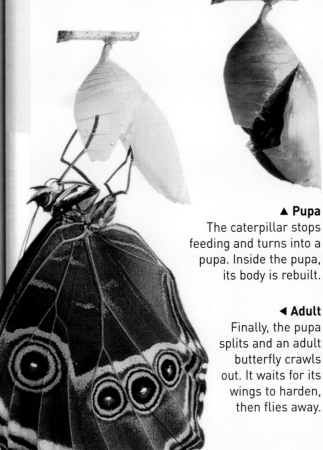

▲ Pupa
The caterpillar stops feeding and turns into a pupa. Inside the pupa, its body is rebuilt.

◄ Adult
Finally, the pupa splits and an adult butterfly crawls out. It waits for its wings to harden, then flies away.

Adult hangs from pupa while its wings harden

WHAT YOU WILL NEED

- Flashlight with flat base
- Oblong cardboard box (at least 25% higher than the flashlight)
- Egg cartons
- Stapler
- Glue stick
- Scissors

Ask an adult to help you cut the box because this can be difficult.

Making a moth trap

Moths cannot resist bright lights, which is why they often come to windows after dark. If you make a moth trap, you can collect moths overnight and examine them during the day. When you open up your trap, you'll be able to see the beautiful camouflaged patterns that many moths use to hide. Moths are completely harmless to people—they cannot sting or bite. Once you have admired them, let them fly away.

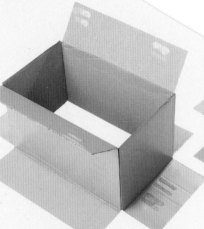

1 **Open all the flaps** of the box. Carefully cut off the top flaps on the shortest sides, leaving the two long ones. Keep the flaps you have cut off to use later.

2 **Take one** of the flaps that you have cut off and cut it into four narrow strips. Staple these to the top of the box, as shown, so they make a valley with a narrow slit about 3/4 in (2 cm) wide.

3 **Put the box** on one end. Remove the tops from the egg cartons and glue the bottoms to the inside of the box at each end. Moths will rest on these once they have flown into the box.

LURED BY LIGHT

No one knows for certain why moths are attracted to light. One theory is that they fly off course, mistaking artificial light for moonlight. Lights attract lots of other insects as well, which means they create great places to go bug-watching.

Light meal ▲
This gecko is lurking near a light, where it will find moths to eat.

MOTHS INDOORS

On summer nights, moths often fly indoors but usually find their way back out. Some moths stay inside all their lives. Clothes moths lay their eggs on anything made of wool. Their caterpillars feed on the wool fibers and leave lots of telltale holes. Adult clothes moths are small, with dusty golden wings. When in danger, they often scuttle into dark corners.

Well wrapped up ▶
These are the caterpillars of the case-bearing clothes moth. Each caterpillar lives inside a portable case, which it makes from silk and short strands of chopped-up wool.

4 **The trap** is now ready. To use it, put it outside after dark. Turn on the flashlight, stand it on end, and carefully place the trap over it. Leave the trap for 1–2 hours, then slowly lift up the box to look at the moths inside.

IMPORTANT

Always ask an adult to come with you to set up the trap after dark. Choose a dry night and put the trap well away from any other bright lights.

Feeding at flowers

People like flowers because they look pretty, but insects like them because they contain food. The food is nectar—a sugary liquid that is packed with energy. In return for the supply of nectar, insects spread pollen from flower to flower, helping plants make their seeds. Flowers are specially shaped to fit particular insect visitors. If you watch bees, butterflies, and hoverflies, you can see which kinds of flowers they visit and which ones they avoid.

Only bees can open toadflax petals to reach inside

Basket containing pollen that the bee has collected

The nectar lies at the bottom of the spur

WHERE TO LOOK

- Bees—on brooms, snapdragons, toadflax, and roses
- Butterflies—on buddleia (butterfly bush), thistles, and valerian
- Hoverflies—on hogweed, elder, and yarrow

Bees
This bumblebee has landed on a toadflax flower and is reaching inside to feed. A bumblebee's tongue is very long and can suck up the nectar in the flower's pointed spur, or nectar tube. As well as drinking nectar, bees also eat pollen. They scrape it off their bodies and press it into special baskets on their legs. When their pollen baskets are full, they fly back to their nest.

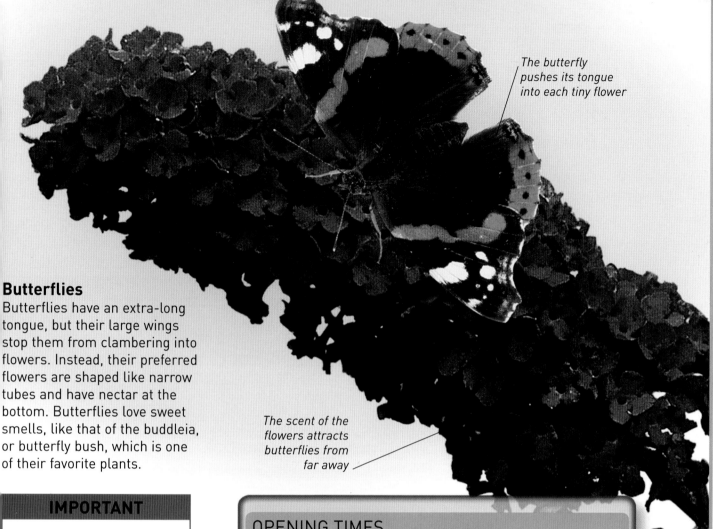

The butterfly pushes its tongue into each tiny flower

The scent of the flowers attracts butterflies from far away

Butterflies

Butterflies have an extra-long tongue, but their large wings stop them from clambering into flowers. Instead, their preferred flowers are shaped like narrow tubes and have nectar at the bottom. Butterflies love sweet smells, like that of the buddleia, or butterfly bush, which is one of their favorite plants.

IMPORTANT

It is safe to use your magnifying glass to watch bees as they feed, but don't get too close or touch them or you might get stung.

Hoverflies

Hoverflies have short tongues, so they cannot reach into deep flowers. Instead, the flowers they visit are often flat. Unlike bees and butterflies, hoverflies are attracted by strong-smelling flowers, often those that are not so nice to a human nose.

OPENING TIMES

Some flowers stay open 24 hours a day, but many open up only when their insect visitors are around. In the early morning, look for flowers that are gradually opening as the air warms up. These flowers stay closed all night but open during the day when bees are on the wing. Some flowers work the other way around. They open up in the evening and stay open all night. These late openers are pollinated by moths, and many give off a sweet scent to help moths track them down.

◀ Night shift
Evening primrose flowers open at night. Their pale color makes them easy for moths to spot in the dark.

Training honeybees

Honeybees are good at finding flowers and remembering where they are. When they get back to their hive, they spread the news by doing a special dance. It shows other bees which direction to fly and how far to go. You can see this system at work by training bees to visit cardboard flowers. Once bees find the flowers, you can test their memories.

WHAT YOU WILL NEED

- Thin cardboard, in five different colors
- Scissors
- Sugar
- Water
- Cup
- Five bottle tops

IMPORTANT

Honeybees can sting. Don't get too close to them when they are feeding. Ask an adult if you or anyone nearby is allergic to bee stings.

Bees arrive to investigate the flowers

1 **Cut out five** cardboard flowers—one of each color. Then mix a solution of sugar and water in a cup.

2 **Put the flowers** outside in the sun and place a bottle top in the center of each one. Put a few drops of sugary water in one of the bottle tops.

DANCING BEES

Bees can't talk and they can't draw maps, but they can tell each other where to find food. When a worker bee finds a patch of flowers, it hurries back to the hive. It crawls onto a honeycomb and carries out a special dance. The round dance tells other workers that the flowers are nearby. The waggle dance shows that they are farther away and tells the other worker bees where to find them.

Message in a dance ▶
The waggle dance works like a compass. The bee dances in a particular direction, waggling its body as it moves. The other bees remember the direction and follow it when they set off from the hive.

INSIDE A BEEHIVE

A honeybee hive is like a busy city, ruled by a single queen. The queen lays all the eggs and keeps the hive under control. The worker bees build the nest, look after the young bee grubs, and forage for food. Honeybees make honey from nectar to feed to their grubs, and they also use it as food in winter. They store it in the honeycombs, putting several drops in each cell before sealing it with a lid.

Bees on a honeycomb ▶
These bees are walking over an empty honeycomb they have just built. The honeycomb is made of wax and contains hundreds of six-sided cells, used for storing honey pollen and raising grubs.

The honeybees lap up the sugar water with their tongues

3 **The first bees** to arrive will report back to their hive. More bees will arrive at the flower that contains food.

4 **Now take away** the sugary water. The bees will remember the flower's color and keep coming back to it, even though there is no food there.

Bees gather at the empty flower expecting to find food

WHAT YOU WILL NEED

- 20 pieces of bamboo cane, about 1/2 in (1 cm) in diameter and 6 in (15 cm) long
- Strong tape
- Modeling clay
- Plant pot

Ask an adult to help you cut the canes to size.

Bee homes

Honeybees live together in hives, but many other garden bees live alone. They lay their eggs in mini-nests and then leave their grubs to grow up on their own. Some of these bees tunnel into wood, but mason bees often nest in hollow plant stems. Solitary bees pollinate many garden plants, so it is worth encouraging them to breed. You can help mason bees to set up home with a flowerpot and some bamboo canes.

LEAFCUTTER BEES

Precision cut ▲
This leafcutter bee is using its sharp jaws to slice a piece out of a rose leaf. When it has finished, it will carry the piece of leaf back to its nest.

In summer, look closely at rose plants and see if you can spot any semicircular holes in their leaves. These holes are made by leafcutter bees—small insects that nest in hollow stems. Unlike mason bees, leafcutters do not line their nests with mud. Instead, they make small parcels from leaves—rose leaves are by far their favorite kind. Each parcel contains a single egg and a supply of pollen for the developing grub to feed on when it emerges.

1 **Stand the pieces** of cane on end to make a bundle. Then bind them together with the tape. Press the canes into a lump of modeling clay to seal one end.

2 **Put the canes** into the plant pot, with the open ends facing outward. Use some more modeling clay to wedge the bundle tightly inside the pot.

CARPENTER BEES

Most solitary bees are small, so they are easy to overlook. Carpenter bees are quite different because some of them are over 1 in (2.5 cm) long. These impressive insects have furry bodies, their wings are often black, and they make a deep buzzing sound when they fly. Most carpenter bees make nests by chewing tunnels in dead wood. The female pats pollen into loaf shapes, lays an egg on each one, and then seals it up.

Big buzzer ▶
Carpenter bees live in warm parts of the world. This great carpenter bee is the largest kind of bee in Australia.

3 **Leave the pot** in a sunny, dry spot. In the spring, mason bees will line the canes with mud and then lay their eggs.

Insect architects

Insects are some of the finest builders in the animal world. Unlike human builders, they do not have to learn how to carry out their work. Instead, their instincts tell them what plan to follow, and what materials to use. Bees often make their nests from wax, but other insects use wood fibers, leaves, or clay. If you look carefully, you may be able to spot insects collecting building materials before heading back to their nests.

The center of the nest contains small cells, where the queen lays her eggs

Crunch time

If you see a wasp sitting still on a wooden post or fence, sneak up on it and listen carefully. Often, you will be able to hear the sound of its jaws crunching up the wood. The color of a wasps' nest depends on the kind of wood they collect.

ANT NESTS

Wood ants ▲
These ants make nests from pine needles and twigs. One nest can contain thousands of ants.

Ants are among the world's most successful insects. They live in forests, grasslands, and towns and cities. Some ants make nests from piles of leaves, but most nest under fallen logs, or underground. If you accidentally disturb an ants' nest, watch how the ants quickly carry their larvae away to safety.

The thin paper walls of the nest look like a series of overlapping shells

Paper homes

Common wasps build their nests from fibers of dead wood. They chew up the fibers, mix them with spit, and then spread them out to make a kind of paper. The queen lays her eggs inside the nest. Worker wasps maintain the nest and enlarge it by building extra walls.

Wasps scrape and chew at the wood, mixing the fibers with their saliva

TERMITE NESTS

Cool homes ▲

Compass termites make flat-sided nests that stay cool when the sun is overhead.

Termites build the biggest nests in the insect world. Some make their nests from wood fibers, but the most impressive nests are made of clay. The clay is soft when the termites build the nest, but it turns hard as it bakes in the sun.

IMPORTANT

Wasps and ants defend their nests fiercely, so keep your distance if you see one, or you risk getting stung or bitten.

On the trail

Ants are hard-working insects, and they scout far and wide in search of food. If one ant discovers something tasty, others soon arrive to help take the food back to the nest. Ants have very bad eyesight but a sharp sense of smell. Wherever they walk, they leave a trail of scent so they never get lost. If you give ants some food, you can see how quickly they sniff it out, spread the news, and carry it back down the trail to their nest.

WHAT YOU WILL NEED

- Crumbs (bread, cookies, cereal, chips, etc.)
- Magnifying glass
- Small stick or stone
- Watch

Worker ants grip the food in their jaws

1 **Look for a trail** of ants in your backyard or garden. When you find one, put some crumbs nearby. Next, put a small stick or stone 3 ft (1 m) back down the trail. When the ants find the food, check the time on your watch.

2 **Stand well back** from the ants and watch them as they carry the food away. When they get past the marker, check the time again. From this, you can tell how long it takes them to travel 3 ft (1 m) carrying their load.

MEETING AND GREETING

If you watch ants on a trail, you will notice that they often touch each other with their antennae when they meet. They do this as an identity check, and also to swap news about food. Every ant has a smell, which it gets from its nest. If an ant meets another ant with the same smell, it knows that it is a friend and is not from a different nest. Ants also smell like the food they collect, so other ants can tell what they have found.

Getting together ▶
These two red ants are touching each other's antennae. They use their antennae to smell each other as well as to test any food that they find.

FLYING ANTS

In warm weather, watch out for flying ants swarming into the air. These winged ants grow up in the safety of the nest, where they are cared for by worker ants. When the weather is right, the workers let them out so they can fly off to start nests of their own. If you see flying ants taking off, look for birds swooping in to enjoy this feast of flying food.

Airborne ▶
These winged ants have crawled up a plant and are taking off. The males die soon after mating. The females shed their wings after they land, and then look for somewhere to make a nest.

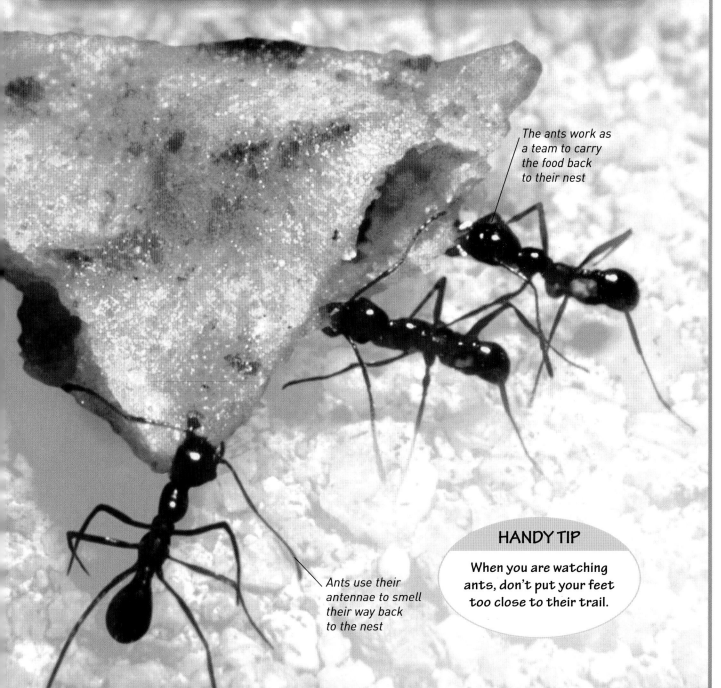

The ants work as a team to carry the food back to their nest

Ants use their antennae to smell their way back to the nest

HANDY TIP

When you are watching ants, don't put your feet too close to their trail.

Friends and enemies

Aphids, or greenflies, are among the fastest-breeding bugs on Earth. They live by sucking sap from plants and are easy to find because they cannot run away. Aphids have lots of enemies, but they are not as helpless as they seem. They are protected by ants, which work like a team of security guards. If you find some aphids, take a closer look. You will often see ants scurrying around them and even over their backs. In return for protection, the ants receive drops of sugary honeydew.

Teaming up

This ant is collecting drops of honeydew from an aphid. Aphids produce honeydew as they feed, and ants collect it and take it to their nests. If any other insects come near the aphids, the ants attack them and chase them away.

The ant touches the aphids with its antennae to make them release honeydew

Aphids have sharp mouthparts so they can pierce plant stems to suck the sap

WHERE TO LOOK

The best time to find aphids is in spring and early summer. They feed near the tips of stems and on the undersides of leaves. These are some of their favorite garden plants:
• Beans
• Fruit trees
• Potatoes
• Roses

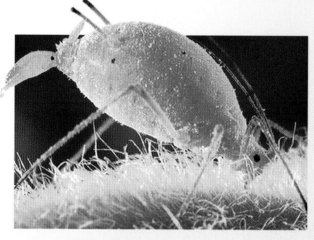

Booming families

Most insects breed by laying eggs, but aphids often give birth to live young. This female is producing a baby while she feeds. In spring and summer, female aphids often have several babies a day. A few weeks later, they are surrounded by many fast-growing young. Unlike most insects, aphids can reproduce without mating.

Aphid eaters

Ladybugs and their grubs are very useful garden insects because they help to keep aphids under control. Other aphid enemies include lacewings and tiny parasitic wasps that lay their eggs inside aphids' bodies. These predators and parasites are not put off by the aphids' security guards.

HONEYDEW

Aphids suck up several times their own weight of sap every day. Once they have digested it, lots of sugar and water is left behind. Aphids get rid of this sugary liquid by producing droplets of honeydew. If you stand under a tree that is full of aphids, you may feel a honeydew mist landing on your face. Honeydew leaves shiny smudges on leaves and sticky blotches on parked cars.

Hungry helpers ▲
If honeydew collects on leaves, it encourages the growth of a mold that is harmful to aphids. Hungry ants prevent this from happening.

Growing a home

Some insect grubs have a clever way of keeping out of sight—they release chemicals that make plants grow them a home. These homes are called galls, and they often look like small buttons or fruit. The grubs live inside the galls and use their juicy flesh as food. When the grubs have grown up, they crawl out and fly away. You can find galls on all kinds of plants, including trees, bushes, and garden weeds. If you collect some galls, you can open them up to see if any grubs are still inside.

WHAT YOU WILL NEED

- Selection of galls from various plants
- Sharp knife
- Cutting board
- Magnifying glass

Ask an adult to help you cut open the galls. Some are hard and must be opened carefully.

1 **Search for galls** on leaves and on the tips of stems and small twigs. Pick the leaf or twig carefully. Oak trees are great places to start looking because many kinds of gall insects live on them.

2 **Look at the gall** to see if you can spot a hole. If there is one, it means that the gall grub has already grown up and flown away. If you cannot see a hole, cut open the gall and you may find a gall grub inside.

Cherry galls develop on the underside of oak leaves

The gall's spongy flesh hides the grub and gives it something to eat

The grub lives in the middle of the gall and feeds on it as it grows up

PLANT PROTECTION

In warm parts of the world, some ants spend all their lives in trees. The ants make their nest in hollow galls, and the tree gives them all the food they need. In return, the ants work like armed guards. If an animal tries to eat the tree's leaves, the ants pour out of their nest. They bite and sting the intruder until it gives up and goes away.

Whistling thorn ▲
This African tree has hollow galls at the base of its thorns. Ants set up home inside them, nibbling a hole to make an entrance. When the wind blows, the galls sometimes make a whistling sound.

Attack from outside

Gall bugs are safe from birds but not from other insects. If you look at galls while they are still on plants, you may sometimes spot flies or wasps laying their eggs inside. Fly grubs eat the gall itself, but wasp grubs are parasites—they feed on the grub that made the gall.

This parasitic wasp lays its eggs in oak marble galls

The wasp bores into the gall with its ovipositor (egg-laying tube)

HANDY TIP

In the fall, look for galls on bare twigs and the underside of fallen leaves.

Oak marble galls look like small wooden fruit

Gall types

Gall bugs are picky about where they live. Each kind lives on just one kind of plant and always makes the same kind of gall. Some galls are soft and do not last for long. Others turn hard and woody as the summer wears on. These hard galls are ideal for collecting and keeping.

Spangle galls ▶
These soft galls grow in clusters on the underside of oak leaves. Each one looks like a small button fastened by a tiny stalk. The wasps that make these galls are just 0.1 in (3 mm) long.

Knopper galls ▶
Instead of growing on leaves, knopper galls grow on acorns. They are easy to spot because they are large and knobby, and they stay on the tree for a long time.

Bedeguar galls ▲
These galls grow on wild roses. The outside of the galls is soft and furry but the inside is hard, like wood. Each gall contains lots of grubs.

Mines and galleries

Some young insects—also called larvae and grubs—live inside leaves and wood. Here, they can munch their way through their food with little danger of being spotted and eaten. It is not easy to find the larvae themselves, but you can look out for the telltale signs that they leave behind. Leaf-eaters often make wiggly mines, while bark beetles dig out tunnels called galleries in dead and dying trees.

The caterpillar left the leaf here

This apple leaf has been mined by the caterpillar of a small moth

Leaf miners

Leaf miners are tiny larvae or grubs that live between the top and bottom surfaces of leaves. As they feed, they move through the leaf, leaving a track called a mine. The mine gets wider as the larva grows, and stops where the larva climbs out to turn into an adult insect.

LOOKING AT LEAF MINES

Leaf miners attack many different plants, but brambles and fruit trees are their particular favorites. If you look at these plants in summer and early fall, the mines are often easy to spot. To get an even better view, collect some leaves with mines and fasten them to the inside of a window with some tape. Because the mines are hollow, they will appear paler than the rest of the leaf. Look carefully at the thickest end of the mine to see if the caterpillar is still inside.

◄ Leaf mines on show
If you make a leaf mine collection, you will be able to see differences in the way the mines are made. Some miners wander all over a leaf. Others stick to one area and chew out a single block.

Leaf miner larva

This leaf miner is chewing its way through an oak leaf. As it feeds, it leaves a trail of droppings in the middle of the mine. The most common kinds of leaf miner are moth caterpillars, but they also include the larvae of beetles and flies.

The mine starts where an adult moth lays an egg

BARK RUBBING

Beetle galleries have lots of interesting patterns because bark beetle larvae dig in different ways. Some galleries have tunnels in parallel lines, while others spread out through the wood like stars. You can record different types by making rubbings with a wax crayon. Find a gallery and brush away any dust or loose wood. Tape a sheet of white paper on top of it, then rub the crayon gently over the paper.

▲ **Making a rubbing**
To make really good rubbings, use a thick crayon and do not press too hard.

Tree galleries

Bark beetle larvae feed on wood, chewing tunnels, or galleries, beneath a tree's bark. To find their galleries, look at dead trees and large pieces of fallen bark. Most galleries are made up of lots of separate tunnels spreading out like slender fingers. Each tunnel is made by a single larva.

Fun with flies

Flies aren't popular insects. Some of them bite, while others buzz around and land on food. But not all flies are troublesome. Fruit flies are tiny and harmless, and they are easy to raise. All you have to do is attract adult flies with some overripe fruit. If you keep the fruit in a warm place, their eggs will turn into adults in just seven days. That's about a thousand times faster than humans grow up!

WHAT YOU WILL NEED

- Overripe banana
- Knife
- Cutting board
- Large jelly jar
- Piece of muslin 4 in (10 cm) square
- Strong elastic band

1 **Chop the banana** into thick slices—there's no need to peel it first.

IMPORTANT

Don't forget to empty the jar when you are finished observing the fruit flies. Dump the contents on to a compost pile if you can.

2 **Put the slices** in the jar and leave the jar in a warm, sunny spot near an open window. Fruit flies will be attracted to the banana and will lay their eggs on it. After 24 hours, cover the top of the jar with the muslin and fasten it with the elastic band. Make a note of the date.

FLY EYES

Fruit flies are only about ⅛ in (5 mm) long, so you need good eyesight to see them on the wing. If you really want to test your vision, try taking a close look at the flies' eyes—they are often brightly colored. Fruit flies have good eyesight, but they find their food mainly by smell. They love things with a fruity or sweet scent, which is why you can often spot them hovering around glasses of fruit juice or wine.

▲ Looking at you
Viewed in close-up, a fruit fly's eyes are striking. They are often bright red or blue.

Problem flies

There are more than 120,000 types of flies in the world, which makes them one of the largest and most important groups of insects. Unlike most other flying insects, true flies have just one pair of wings. Many flies are harmless, but some of them are serious pests.

Housefly ▲
This fly is one of the world's most widespread insects. Adult houseflies feed on anything sweet, using spongelike mouthparts. They dribble on their food when they eat, and can spread germs on their feet.

Mosquito ▲
Male mosquitoes eat nectar, but females feed by sucking blood. The females have sharp mouthparts that pierce skin like a syringe. Most types are harmless, although their bites itch. But some spread diseases, such as malaria.

3 **Look at the jar** every day over the next two weeks. Note the date when they hatch. How long did it take for them to hatch?

Adult fruit flies suck up sugary juices from rotting fruit

Horsefly ▲
Horseflies feed on blood and have a painful bite. Their sharp jaws cut skin open and make it bleed. These flies can be a problem for horses, other farm animals, and even people.

Soaking up the sun

Unlike humans, insects need warmth to stay on the move. On hot days, they move around at top speed. This makes them difficult to follow and even harder to catch. But if it gets cold, they move much more slowly or even come to a stop. If you are bug-watching, one of the best times to study insects is when the sun is coming up in the morning. In the strengthening light, lots of insects sunbathe to get their bodies warm.

WHERE TO LOOK

- Insects warming up— the tops of plants; on bare ground facing the morning sunshine
- Insects cooling down— shaded places; where the soil is damp
- Insects hibernating— under bark and stones; in garages and barns

Sunbathing beauty
This morpho butterfly has opened its wings wide to soak up the warmth of the sun. Its wings work like solar panels, collecting lots of heat. Later in the day, when the air is warm, the butterfly will rest with its wings closed, making it harder to spot.

The butterfly's wings collect warmth and carry it toward its body. Dark areas are good at absorbing heat

SPEEDING UP

Warmth doesn't only make insects move faster—it also makes them grow up more quickly. If the temperature is 59 °F (15 °C), a bluebottle can take seven weeks to grow up and lay its eggs. But if the temperature is 86 °F (30 °C), it can speed through its life cycle in just 16 days. This is why summer is the busiest time for bugs.

Growing up ▶
Bluebottle maggots feed for just over a week before turning into pupae. If the weather is hot, the adult flies emerge three or four days later. Soon, they are ready to breed.

Adult bluebottle ▶
If the warm weather lasts, an adult bluebottle can become a great-great-grandparent in just two months. But when the weather turns cold, the flies stop breeding, and their numbers start to fall.

Bluebottle larvae ▼
Bluebottles, or blowflies, lay their eggs on meat. In hot weather, the eggs hatch in less than a day. The fly's larvae, or maggots, immediately start to feed.

Hibernation
In winter, hardly any insects are on the wing. Most of them are hibernating until warmer times return. Many spend the winter as eggs or larvae, but some hibernate as adults. Ladybugs hibernate in hollow tree trunks, rocks, or other shelters. Many other insects hibernate under bark.

Freshwater insects

Ponds and streams are great places to watch insects. Pond skaters skim across the surface, while all kinds of bugs and creepy crawlies swim beneath it. Some of these insects are full-time water animals, but many leave the water when they have grown up. Freshwater insects are easy to catch with a net, but you can watch many of them with no equipment at all. Just wait quietly by the water's edge and watch them come to the surface to breathe.

Back legs work like rudders, steering the pond skater from behind

Pond skater skimming on water surface

Feet spread the pond skater's weight over the surface film

Front legs detect ripples from drowning insects

TESTING SURFACE TENSION

To find out why pond skaters don't sink, try this simple experiment. Fill a bowl with water and wait until the surface is completely still. Next, pick up a small paper clip with a pair of tweezers and gently lower it on to the water. Because the paper clip is light, it will sit on the water's surface film. Pond skaters float in exactly the same way.

◄ Floating paper clips
Surface tension gives water a filmy surface. It can hold up light objects, such as a paper clip, but anything heavy breaks through it and sinks.

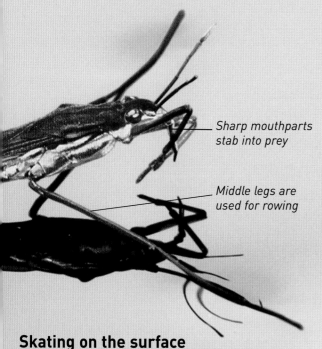

Sharp mouthparts stab into prey

Middle legs are used for rowing

Skating on the surface

Pond skaters are carnivorous bugs that literally walk on water. They have water-repellent feet, and they skate on the surface film, which keeps them high and dry. Pond skaters pounce on other insects that have crash-landed, stabbing them with their jaws.

Leaving the water

After two years underwater, this young damselfly has climbed out to start adult life. It sheds its skin for a final time and then unfolds it wings so that it can fly away. To see this amazing transformation, visit a pond on a still summer morning. This is when most damselflies and dragonflies emerge.

UP AND AWAY

Water boatmen underwater ▲

Most underwater insects have wings and some are powerful fliers. Water boatmen, like the two shown here, often fly from pond to pond when the weather is warm. To see this for yourself, use a net to catch one and then put it on the ground. Be careful not to touch it because it may bite. If it cannot scuttle back into the water, it will wait until it is dry and then suddenly take to the air and fly away.

Coming up for air

Old water tanks and cattle troughs are good places for seeing how freshwater insects breathe. Mosquito larvae use tiny snorkels. They will dive down when they see you approach, but come back up in a few minutes.

Spiders

Many people don't like spiders—especially ones that have long, hairy legs. But spiders are fascinating animals, and they help us a lot by keeping bugs under control. Unlike insects, spiders always live by hunting, and insects make up most of their prey. Some spiders stalk their victims, but many ambush them or trap them in silken webs. Next time you see a spider, take a closer look. Lots of spidery eyes will be looking back at you.

IMPORTANT

Some spiders have a dangerous bite or tiny hairs that get into your skin. To be safe, never pick up a spider with bare hands.

Spider basics

This male house spider has just caught a fly. Like all spiders, it has eight legs and a pair of venomous fangs. Its mouth is tiny, so instead of chewing its food, it has to suck it up. House spiders have four pairs of eyes. They find their prey by sight and also by touch.

Four pairs of eyes give the spider an all-round view

Body is made of two parts—the head and the cephalothorax

Fangs stab into the prey to inject venom

Once the fly is dead, the spider squirts digestive juices into it to make it edible

HIDDEN SPIDERS

Spiders are easy to spot when they scuttle across the ground. But lots of spiders take care not to be seen. If you look carefully at bark and among leaves, you will often find spiders that are beautifully camouflaged. The world's biggest spiders hide in burrows and come out to feed at night.

Into the open ▲
This nocturnal tarantula comes out of its home in a tree hole to hunt.

Long legs covered with sensitive hairs that detect tiny vibrations from other animals

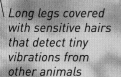

Spiders' legs end in small pads or claws

Spider parade

There are more than 40,000 kinds of spider in the world, and they come in many shapes and sizes. Look out for these common kinds—they often live in gardens, backyards, or indoors.

Crab spider ▶
These colorful spiders lurk among flowers and catch insects as they land to feed. Although they are only about $3/4$ in (2 cm) long, their venom is powerful enough to kill bumblebees and butterflies.

◀ Jumping spider
Jumping spiders have large front eyes. They hunt by day, watching for tiny animals and leaping on them. They often have striped bodies and short legs.

Orb-web spider ▶
These common spiders catch flying insects in their circular webs. The largest orb-web spiders live in warm parts of the world and make webs over 3 ft (1 m) across.

◀ Grass spider
Grass spiders have long bodies and four pairs of small, forward-facing eyes. If they are threatened, they often stretch out along a twig or a blade of grass to hide.

Web watch

Orb-weaver spiders are some of the best builders in the animal world. Their webs are tough and efficient, thanks to the stretchiness of the silk and the way they are designed. One of the best ways to investigate webs is to make one yourself. If you use elastic, rather than string, your web will stay in shape just like the real thing.

WHAT YOU WILL NEED

- Wooden board 20 in (50 cm) square
- Colored paper 24 in (60 cm) square
- Scissors
- Adhesive tape
- Simple ring, key ring, or narrow washer
- 13 ft (4 m) flat elastic braid, 1/4 in (5 mm) wide
- 12 colored thumbtacks or map pins
- Reel of fine elastic thread, at least 33 ft (10 m) long

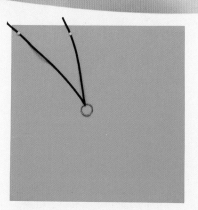

1 **Cover the board** with paper and put the washer in the middle. Pass a piece of braid through it and pin both ends to the edge of the board to make the first two spokes. Make sure the braid is pulled tight, then trim the loose ends.

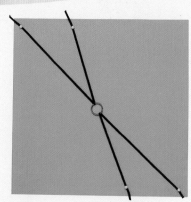

2 **Make another pair** of spokes opposite the first, adjusting the braid so that it is tight and the washer is still in the middle. Then pin the braid in place and trim it as before.

Spiders glue the spiral to the spokes, but the model web uses knots instead

MAKING SILK

If you look at a spider with a magnifying glass, you will be able to see how it makes silk. The silk comes out of nozzles called spinnerets, like toothpaste squirting out of a tube. It hardens as it meets the air, turning into stretchy strands. Most spiders make dry silk to build the spokes of their webs and sticky silk to connect them together.

Starting out ▶
This spider is producing strands of dry silk, which will make up the framework of its web.

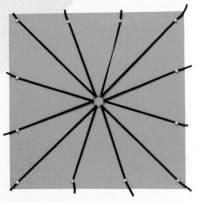 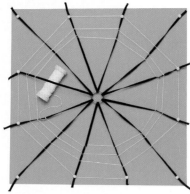

3 **Working on alternate** sides of the board, put the remaining spokes in place. Remember to keep the braid tight so that the washer stays in the center of the board.

4 **Starting at the center**, make a spiral with the elastic. Wind it around each spoke in turn and keep it taut.

Web types

If you ask someone to draw a spiderweb, they will probably draw an orb web. But spiders make many different kinds of web. See how many of these you can spot.

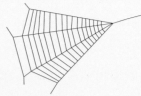

Triangular web ▲
Triangle-web spiders make webs with four spokes. They sit on a twig holding a line to keep the web taut.

Hammock web ▲
Hammock-web spiders spin a silk sheet, to which they add a tangle of fine silk lines. Insects get caught in these lines.

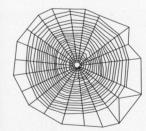

Orb web ▲
Some orb-web spiders spin webs with a patch or zig-zag of silk at the center, where they wait for their prey.

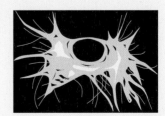

Funnel web ▲
Funnel-web spiders make webs that spread out like a funnel from their lair. These webs are often found in corners or between stones.

Real orb webs often have a ring at the center

5 **When you have** finished, pin down the end of the thread. The tension in the elastic will keep the web in shape.

Good vibrations

Although they have lots of eyes, most spiders cannot see well. Instead, they rely on touch to tell when an insect has landed on their web. The struggling insect makes the web vibrate. The spider senses the vibrations and rushes across the web to grab its prey. With the help of a blade of grass—or better still, a tuning fork—you can sometimes trick a spider into thinking it has caught a meal.

WHAT YOU WILL NEED

- Blade of grass or tuning fork

⚠ Be careful not to tear any webs.

HOW SPIDERS FEED

Spiders have tiny mouths so they cannot chew their prey. Instead, they squirt digestive juices into their victims to dissolve the soft parts. The spider then sucks up this juicy mixture, leaving a dried-out husk. Before they feed, many web-building spiders wrap up their prey in silk. Some leave the corpse on their web, but many snip it free and carry it back to their lair.

Packaged food ▲
This garden orb-web spider has caught a small insect and is wrapping it in silk.

Touchy moment
Pick a blade of grass and tap it on a spiderweb so that the tip vibrates. If you vibrate it fast enough, the spider will mistake it for a buzzing insect and will rush across the web. The moment you stop tapping, the spider will stop, too. To try this with a tuning fork, tap the prongs against something hard to make the fork ring. Gently touch the base of the fork against the web.

TRAPDOOR SPIDERS

In warm parts of the world, look out for silk triplines on the ground. These belong to trapdoor spiders, which live in burrows with camouflaged lids. Trapdoor spiders use these triplines to sense their prey. If an insect accidentally brushes against one of them, the spider flings open the lid of its burrow and runs out to catch its meal. If you spot a trapdoor, try lifting it with a twig. The spider will hide at the bottom of its burrow or make an emergency escape.

Opening time ▶
This trapdoor spider has sensed movement and is rushing out to catch its prey.

Hanging by a thread

When spiders move around, they leave a line of silk behind them. It is called a dragline, and it lets spiders drop safely through the air, or even glide away. A spider's dragline is often so fine that it is hard to see, but it is easily strong enough to support the spider's weight. If you persuade a spider to take a jump, you will be able to see its dragline in action. Unlike a reel of thread, it never gets tangled up and it never runs out.

WHAT YOU WILL NEED

- Jelly jar
- Piece of stiff paper
- Spider
- Watercolor paintbrush

Tip the jar gently so that the spider isn't taken by surprise

1 **Use the jelly jar** and paper to catch a small spider. Try looking on walls outside and in corners indoors.

2 **Turn the jar** upright and give it a gentle shake to make the spider fall to the bottom. Then you can remove the paper from the top of the jar.

3 **Pick up** the brush. Hold the jar at shoulder height and gradually turn it on its side. Use the brush to edge the spider out of the jar.

4 **The spider** will drop into the air, lowering itself on its dragline. It can stop at any point by shutting down its spinnerets, and can climb back up its dragline.

IMPORTANT

Do the dragline test outside if you do not want the spider to escape indoors. Don't touch the spider with your hands or it may bite you.

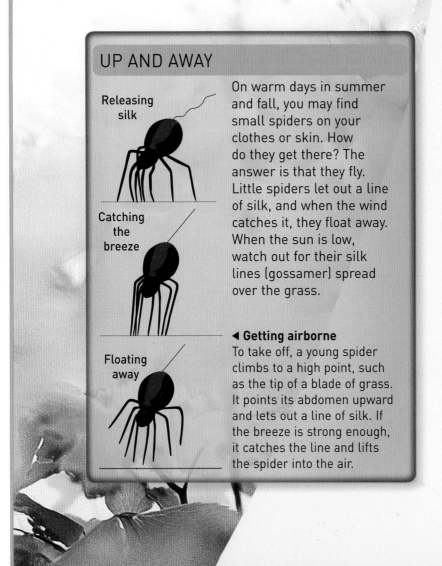

UP AND AWAY

Releasing silk

Catching the breeze

Floating away

On warm days in summer and fall, you may find small spiders on your clothes or skin. How do they get there? The answer is that they fly. Little spiders let out a line of silk, and when the wind catches it, they float away. When the sun is low, watch out for their silk lines (gossamer) spread over the grass.

◄ Getting airborne
To take off, a young spider climbs to a high point, such as the tip of a blade of grass. It points its abdomen upward and lets out a line of silk. If the breeze is strong enough, it catches the line and lifts the spider into the air.

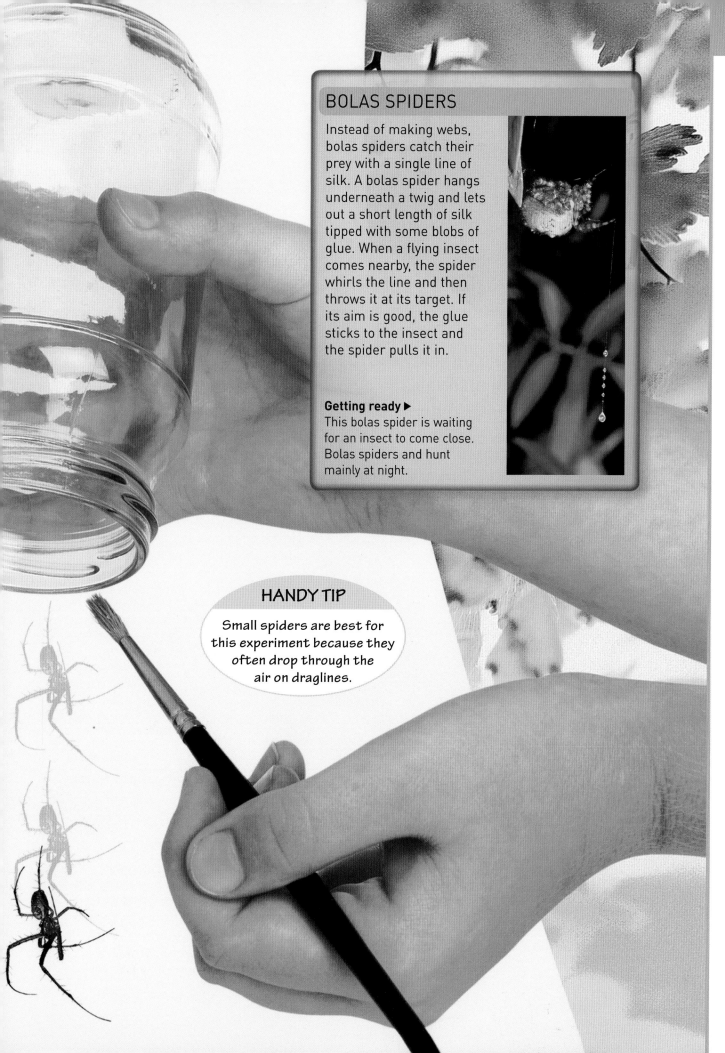

BOLAS SPIDERS

Instead of making webs, bolas spiders catch their prey with a single line of silk. A bolas spider hangs underneath a twig and lets out a short length of silk tipped with some blobs of glue. When a flying insect comes nearby, the spider whirls the line and then throws it at its target. If its aim is good, the glue sticks to the insect and the spider pulls it in.

Getting ready ▶
This bolas spider is waiting for an insect to come close. Bolas spiders and hunt mainly at night.

HANDY TIP

Small spiders are best for this experiment because they often drop through the air on draglines.

Spiders without webs

All spiders make silk, but only some of them use webs to catch food. Many other kinds hunt by lurking in flowers or by searching out their prey. These roaming hunters include spiders that get stuck in bathtubs, as well as huge tropical tarantulas that feed on lizards and even birds. Some of these spiders are true wanderers, but most build themselves a lair. When they are finished hunting, they go home and hide.

SPIDERS IN THE BATH

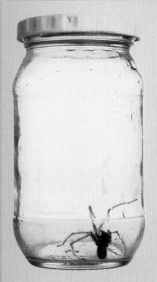

◄ Spider rescue
If you find a spider trapped in the tub, don't wash it away. Instead, use a jelly jar and a piece of paper to catch it and put it outside. Put the jar over the spider, then slide the paper underneath. Turn the jar upright, then take away the paper and replace it with the jar lid.

Bathrooms are great places for spotting spiders, which often suddenly appear in tubs and sinks, giving people a nasty shock. But how do they get there, and why? Despite what you may have heard, spiders definitely don't come up out of the drain. They fall in while they are looking for food or for a mate. Once they are in, they are trapped because their feet cannot get a grip on a tub or sink's shiny sides.

Spider's bright color may be easy for a human to spot, but it is not so easy for an insect to see

Lurking in flowers

If you see a bee or a butterfly that seems stuck to a flower, take a closer look. It's very likely that it has been caught by a crab spider. Crab spiders lurk in flowers with their front legs held out like a crab's claws. If an insect lands, the spider snaps shut its legs to grab its prey.

Ground hunters

Many spiders hunt on the ground. This wolf spider is a daytime hunter and it uses speed to catch its prey. It runs over the soil and up small plants, catching anything that comes its way.

A tarantula's feet are covered with short hairs, which give the spider a good sense of touch

Hunting at night

The world's biggest spiders are tarantulas. They are ground-based hunters, although they sometimes climb trees. Unlike wolf spiders, they creep around after dark, using their legs to feel for food.

Downward-pointing fangs pin the spider's prey to the ground when it attacks

LOOK HERE!

Jumping spiders are small, perky creatures, which often walk over fences and walls. They have good eyesight, and they jump like tiny acrobats, landing on their prey. If you find a jumping spider on a wall or paving stone, hold an upright pencil an inch or so away. Move the pencil in a circle around the spider. The spider will turn around to watch the pencil moving and may even look up to glance at you.

◄ **Double take**
Unlike other spiders, jumping spiders are not afraid of people. Using their big front eyes, they will take a good look at anything you put in their way.

Family life

Compared to insects, spiders are careful parents. Female spiders often guard their eggs, and some of them even carry their young on their backs. The young spiders stay aboard their mother for several days until they are ready to start life on their own. But before any of this can happen, parent spiders have to get together and mate. For the male spider, mating can be a dangerous business. If he moves too fast or gives off the wrong signals, the female may attack him and turn him into a meal.

Him or her?

In the spider world, females are often much bigger than males. Here, a male black widow looks tiny compared with his vastly bigger mate. If you see a small spider approaching a much larger one on a web, it may well be a courting couple.

Male waves his palps up and down in a set sequence, while creeping toward the female

Careful approach

This male wolf spider is signaling to a female so that he can approach her and safely mate. He does this by waving his palps, which look like a pair of arms. Web-building spiders use a different system. The male signals by giving the female's web some sharp tugs.

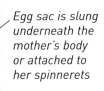

Egg sac is slung underneath the mother's body or attached to her spinnerets

Precious packages

Female spiders wrap their eggs inside a cocoon, or sac made of silk. Some bury their egg sacs underground, but many fasten them to plants or hide them in crevices indoors. Wolf spiders carry their egg sacs with them as they move around.

SCATTER

When garden spiders hatch, they have to look after themselves. They cluster together in a ball on a special nursery web. If you spot one, gently tap it with a pencil. The ball will seem to explode as the spiders scatter. They will soon come back together, and the ball will reappear. This scattering trick helps to protect the spider from birds.

Run for it ▶
These hatchlings are scattering in all directions after being touched.

All aboard

When wolf spiders hatch, they climb on to their mother and cluster around her back. She carries them wherever she goes. The baby spiders do not feed, but they stay on her back until they are ready to shed their skins. Once they have done that, they wander off to start hunting food.

Young spiders link legs to form a living jacket around the female's body, keeping well clear of her legs

WHAT YOU WILL NEED

- Tray with a raised edge
- White paper or paper towel
- Swing-arm lamp
- Plastic bag
- Trowel
- Magnifying glass

Life in leaf litter

When leaves fall to the ground, they turn into a crumbly compost called leaf litter. This underfoot world is a great place for bug-hunting because it's full of mini-insects and creepy-crawlies. Leaf litter animals live in a world that is damp and dark, and they normally stay hidden beneath the surface. But if you collect some leaf litter and shine a bright light on it, they will scuttle for cover, making them easy to see.

Fallen leaves provide food for many kinds of leaf litter animals

Dead remains are eaten by beetles and other scavengers

MINI SCORPIONS

Pseudoscorpions are some of the most common animals in leaf litter. However, they are so tiny that you need really sharp eyes to spot them. These bugs look just like tiny scorpions, but the good news is they don't have stingers. Pseudoscorpions use their pincers to catch other animals. Their pincers also come in handy for hitching a ride aboard insects—an easy way of getting around.

Predator with pincers ▶
Pseudoscorpions have slender pincers, pear-shaped bodies, and eight legs. Most are less than $\frac{1}{8}$ in (3 mm) long.

1 **Collect some leaf litter** with the trowel and put it in a plastic bag. Get plenty of damp leaves because the dry ones on top contain far fewer animals.

2 **Back home,** cover the tray with clean white paper. Put a handful of leaf litter in the middle of the tray and spread it so it forms a thin layer.

3 **Position the lamp** about 12 in (30 cm) above the tray and turn it on. The bright light and warmth will make animals move out of the litter. Once they are on the paper you can look at them closely with a magnifying glass.

4 **When you have finished** looking, take the tray outside and scatter the leaf litter and bugs in a shady place.

Fungi and bacteria help to break down the leaves, turning them into small fragments

Leaf litter critters

All kinds of bugs live in leaf litter. Some are vegetarians that feed on rotting leaves. Others are hunters that wriggle or creep through the leaf litter, finding their prey by touch. See how many of these bugs you can find.

Springtail ▶
These tiny animals have a "spring" under their bodies. They use it to flick themselves away from danger.

Rove beetle ▶
Beetles are common insects in leaf litter. Rove beetles hunt prey and also scavenge dead remains.

◀ Millipede
Millipedes nibble away at dead leaves, fungi, and rotting wood. They often coil up if they are touched.

Earwig ▶
With their long pincers, earwigs are easy to recognize. They feed on leaves and other insects.

Woodlouse ▶
Woodlice eat decaying leaves and fragments of rotting wood. Unlike insects, they have to stay damp to survive.

◀ Centipede
Unlike millipedes, centipedes have flat bodies. They can squeeze into tight spaces to hide or to search for their prey.

MAKE A CHOICE CHAMBER FOR BUGS AND SEE WHAT CONDITIONS THEY PREFER

WHAT YOU WILL NEED

- Two empty fruit juice cartons
- Marker pen
- Scissors
- Stapler and staples
- Strong tape
- Piece of thin cardboard to make the lid
- Paper towels
- Cotton balls
- Water
- Woodlice and a spider

Decisions, decisions

If you make a choice chamber, you can see what conditions attract bugs and what they avoid. The chamber has two rooms connected by a narrow slit. You can adjust the conditions in each room (for example, by making one darker than the other) and leave the bugs to decide which they prefer. Woodlice are good animals for this test. Their brains are small, but they know what suits them best. You can also try repeating the activity using a spider.

1 **Draw a line** around each carton, 2 in (5 cm) from the base. Cut along the lines and staple the bottoms of the cartons together.

2 **Cut an opening** between the two cartons, reaching down to the base. The opening should be no more than $1/2$ in (1 cm) wide. Seal the gap with a strip of tape.

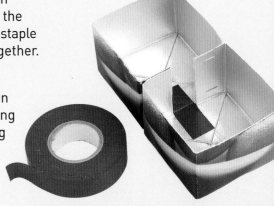

BRAINY BUGS

Some bugs can behave in surprisingly clever ways. Digger wasps, for example, are very good at finding their burrows. They do it by remembering every detail of the ground nearby. These wasps have another, even more impressive trick. When they make a burrow, they often pack down the entrance with a tiny stone. Apart from mammals and birds, very few animals use tools of any kind. For a tiny insect, it is a remarkable skill.

Homing in ▲
Digger wasps nest on the ground in open, sandy soil. They need an exceptional memory to find their way back to their nest.

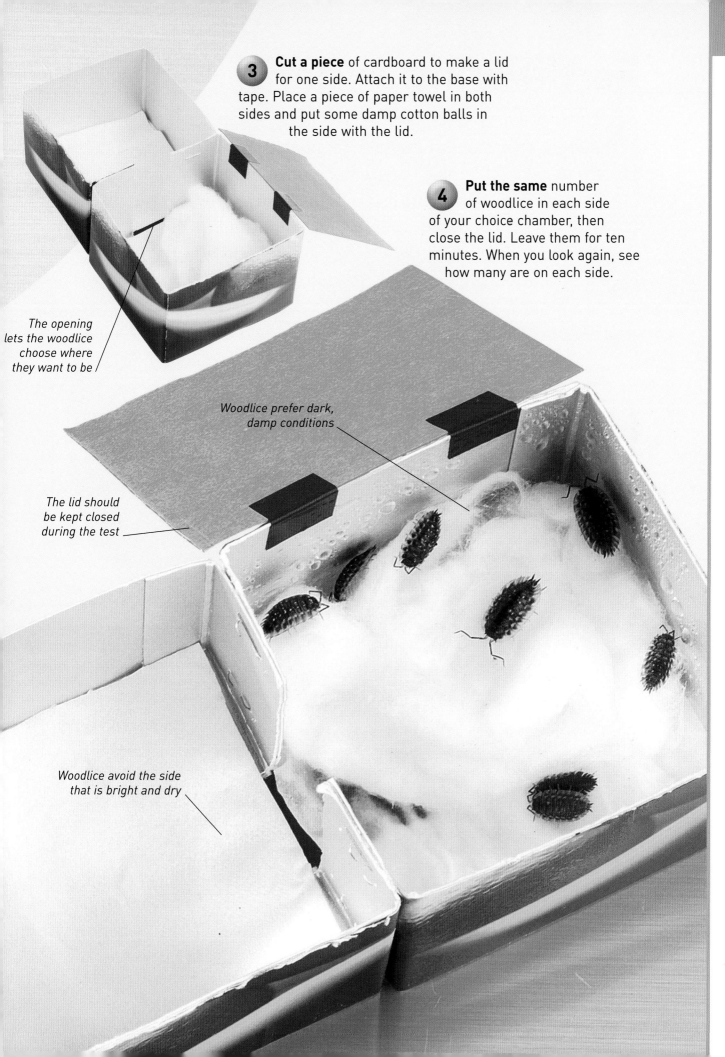

3 Cut a piece of cardboard to make a lid for one side. Attach it to the base with tape. Place a piece of paper towel in both sides and put some damp cotton balls in the side with the lid.

4 Put the same number of woodlice in each side of your choice chamber, then close the lid. Leave them for ten minutes. When you look again, see how many are on each side.

The opening lets the woodlice choose where they want to be

Woodlice prefer dark, damp conditions

The lid should be kept closed during the test

Woodlice avoid the side that is bright and dry

Earthworms

Apart from insects, earthworms are some of the most important animals in the world. By burrowing through the soil, they mix it up and help plants to grow. Earthworms look soft and squishy, but they are very good at tunneling through the soil. To find out how they do it, pick one up and hold it in your closed-up hand. The worm will squeeze its way between your fingers, just as it squeezes through soil tunnels underground.

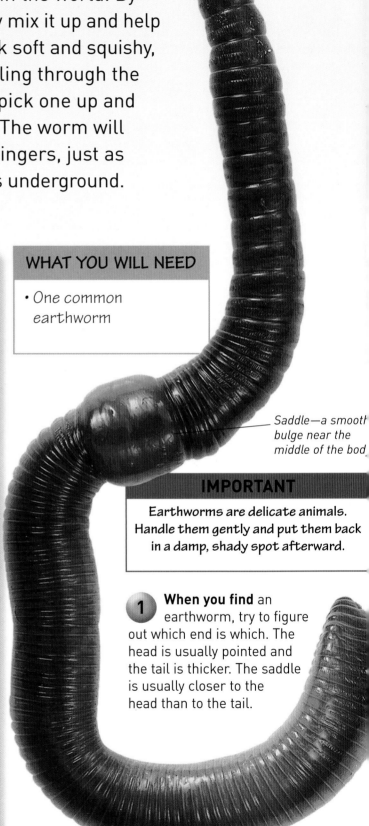

Body is made of muscular rings called segments

Saddle—a smooth bulge near the middle of the body

AMOROUS EARTHWORMS

Earthworms spend almost all their lives underground. The one time they stay on the surface is in late spring and early summer, when they are searching for a mate. They usually come out on warm, damp nights. If you want to see them, take a flashlight covered with a piece of red plastic, because worms react less to red light. Walk carefully, because they can sense vibrations and quickly disappear underground.

Earthworm embrace ▲
When earthworms mate, they lie side by side and cover themselves in sticky mucus.

WHAT YOU WILL NEED

• One common earthworm

IMPORTANT

Earthworms are delicate animals. Handle them gently and put them back in a damp, shady spot afterward.

1 **When you find** an earthworm, try to figure out which end is which. The head is usually pointed and the tail is thicker. The saddle is usually closer to the head than to the tail.

EMERGENCY ESCAPE

When earthworms are on or near the surface, they are at risk from hungry birds. To avoid being eaten, they have to be alert. They do not have true eyes, so they cannot see danger. Instead, they rely on their sense of touch. An earthworm's skin is full of sensitive nerves. If a bird touches a worm's tail, the worm immediately contracts its body. With luck, it gets underground before the bird can pull it out.

Earthworm breakfast ▲
This thrush has caught an earthworm and is about to swallow its meal. Birds find earthworms partly by sight, and also by listening for the faint sounds they make as they tunnel through the soil.

2 **Pick up** the worm and hold it gently by its tail. Its head will move around and its body will start to lengthen as it tries to reach the ground.

At first, the segments are short and fat

The worm pushes its way through any gaps

4 **Finally, put** the worm in your hand and gently close your fingers. It will try to squeeze out. You may be surprised by its strength.

3 **Allow the worm** to relax its body segments. It can double or even triple its length in this way. Worms stretch like this when they burrow and when they crawl over the ground.

The segments relax, becoming longer and thinner

Building a wormery

Earthworms are normally hidden away, so it's difficult to find out how they live. But if you make a wormery, you can peer into their private world. The wormery shown here contains a narrow slice of soil, which makes the worms easy to see. If you build up the soil in contrasting layers, you will be able to watch how the worms mix it up and drag dead leaves underground. As they tunnel, they let air into the soil and help rainwater to drain away.

Ask an adult to help you cut the wood and plastic to size and drill the holes

Don't leave any gaps or your wormery will leak

Don't pack down the soil; leave it loose

1 **Cut the pieces** of wood to size. Use the drill to make three equally spaced holes along both short sides of each sheet of plastic and three holes along one of the long sides of each sheet.

2 **Use these holes** to screw the plastic sheets onto the three pieces of wood that make up the frame. Then screw the two smallest pieces of wood to the base of the frame to make the feet.

3 **Fill the frame** with layers of different-colored soils and sand to about 2 in (5 cm) from the top. Add a layer of leaves and a sprinkle of water to make the soil damp, but not wet. Put in the worms, then cover the wormery with a dark cloth and put it in a cool, dark place.

WORM CASTS

In spring, the ground is often covered with little piles of soil, which look like toothpaste squeezed out of a tube. These are worm casts, and they are soil that has passed through a worm's body. If you see lots of worm casts, it's a sign of fertile soil.

Surface signs ▶
Some worms make casts on the surface, but others leave them underground.

HOW EARTHWORMS FEED

Earthworms feed by swallowing soil and digesting any dead remains that it contains. The rest of the soil travels straight through them and is left behind as a cast. Some worms come to the surface at night and drag dead leaves underground. They nibble away parts of them and leave the rest to fertilize the soil.

Collecting trip ▶
Earthworms collect leaves by holding them in their mouths and pulling them into their tunnels.

IMPORTANT

Don't let your wormery dry out, or the worms will die. When the wormery is full of tunnels, put the worms back where you found them.

4 **Check** your wormery every day and keep the soil damp. After a few days, you will see tunnels as the earthworms eat through the soil.

The soil will get mixed up by the tunneling worms

Helping bugs

Like all other animals, bugs live in a world that is changing fast. Many kinds are affected by pollution. Others are in trouble because their homes are being built on, plowed up, or cut down. Some bugs are also harmed by collectors who gather them from the wild to sell as souvenirs. But the news isn't all bad because plenty of people are working hard to protect endangered bugs and help them survive. If you like bugs, you can do your part to help. Here are some good ways to start.

Keeping bugs

Bugs can make fascinating pets, but before you buy them, ask where they came from. If they were raised in captivity, you will not be doing any harm. If they were not, buying them will encourage people to collect more from the wild.

Many bugs live in or near fresh water, so a pond is a good place to do some bug research

WHAT YOU CAN DO

- Find out if there is a natural history museum near you and visit it.
- Look on the Internet or in your local telephone directory to find contact details for any bug organizations in your area.
- Visit an insect zoo to see living insects from all over the world.
- Tell your friends about bugs and bug-hunting. They can help as well.

Join a bug club

One of the best ways to help bugs is to join a bug club. Many bug societies run clubs for younger members. You can find out about them on the Internet. Bug clubs organize bug-watching forays and they will also answer questions about any bugs that you find.

Visit an insect zoo

A great place to go to find out more about bugs is an insect zoo. Zoos breed their own bugs and they often raise some of the biggest and most exciting insects in the world. Many also have special houses for watching bugs that come out after dark.

BUG SOUVENIRS

In some parts of the world, colorful butterflies are sold as souvenirs. They look beautiful and they don't harm wild butterflies—as long as they have been bred on butterfly farms. But it's not always easy to tell where souvenir bugs have come from, or how they ended up in a shop. To be on the safe side, it's best to leave these souvenirs alone. If you want to see a butterfly collection, visit a local museum.

Studying butterflies ▶
Many museums have butterfly collections. Scientists use them to study butterfly biology and to decide how different kinds should be classified. The scientists also study butterflies in the wild.

Bug classification There are at least a million species of insects in the world, together with lots of other kinds of bugs. Scientists classify them into different groups based on key features that they share.

INSECT	NAME OF GROUP	SPECIES TOTAL	KEY FEATURES	EXAMPLES
Ground beetle	BEETLES **Coleoptera**	370,000	Beetles have hardened front wings that fit over their hind wings like a case. They live on land and in freshwater in most parts of the world, and eat all kinds of food.	Stag beetle Burying beetle Ladybug
Dragonfly	DRAGONFLIES AND DAMSELFLIES **Odonata**	5,500	These large-eyed insects have long bodies and two pairs of filmy wings. As adults, they hunt other insects while on the wing.	Emperor dragonfly Green darner Azure damselfly
Housefly	FLIES **Diptera**	122,000	Flies are the only flying insects with a single pair of wings. Most adult flies feed on liquids, but some eat pollen from flowers.	Housefly Crane fly
Cicada	BUGS **Hemiptera**	82,000	True bugs feed on plants or animals, using their sharp mouthparts to pierce their food. They have two pairs of wings.	Cicada Giant water bug Pond skater
Cricket	CRICKETS AND GRASSHOPPERS **Orthoptera**	20,000	These stout-bodied insects have powerful hind legs and are good at jumping. Most also have two pairs of wings, but some have tiny wings and cannot fly.	Speckled bushcricket Desert locust
Cockroach	COCKROACHES **Blattodea**	4,000	Cockroaches are large, flat-bodied insects that sometimes feed indoors. They have powerful legs and can run away from danger.	American cockroach Madagascan hissing cockroach
Butterfly	BUTTERFLIES AND MOTHS **Lepidoptera**	165,000	These insects are covered with tiny scales. The adults feed on nectar and other sugary liquids, and coil up their mouthparts when not in use.	Monarch butterfly Hawkmoth
Wasp	BEES, WASPS, AND ANTS **Hymenoptera**	108,000	All these insects have slender waists, and many of them also have stingers. Most have two pairs of wings joined by tiny hooks, but worker ants are wingless.	Honeybee Bumblebee Common wasp

On the left, you can find out about some of the most important groups of insects. For other bugs and creepy-crawlies, look below. The species totals show the number that have been identified so far.

INSECT	NAME OF GROUP	SPECIES TOTAL	KEY FEATURES	EXAMPLES
Centipede	CENTIPEDES **Chilopoda**	3,000	Centipedes are long, flat-bodied animals with lots of legs. They are fast-moving hunters, and attack their prey with their poisonous claws.	Giant centipede
Millipede	MILLIPEDES **Diplopoda**	8,000	Millipedes resemble centipedes, but they have four legs on each segment of their bodies instead of two. They feed on plant remains.	Giant millipede
Woodlouse	CRUSTACEANS **Crustacea**	40,000	Crustaceans have hard body cases and several pairs of legs. Most of them live in water, but some kinds live in damp places on land.	Woodlouse
Spider	SPIDERS **Araneae**	40,000	Spiders are eight-legged predators with venomous fangs and several pairs of eyes. Many kinds make silk webs to catch their prey.	Garden orb-web spider Tarantula
Harvestman	DADDY LONGLEGS **Opiliones**	5,000	Daddy longlegs look similar to spiders, but have slender legs and oval bodies without a waist. Unlike spiders, they never make webs.	Daddy longlegs
Mite	TICKS AND MITES **Acari**	30,000	These eight-legged animals feed on a wide variety of food. Ticks suck blood, but mites attack both plants and animals.	Sheep tick House dust mite
Scorpion	SCORPIONS **Scorpiones**	1,400	Scorpions are flat-bodied animals with four pairs of legs, two pincers, and a tail that has a venomous sting.	Imperial scorpion
Pseudo-scorpion	PSEUDO-SCORPIONS **Pseudoscorpiones**	33,000	These tiny scorpion-like animals often live in leaf litter. Unlike true scorpions, they do not have a stinger.	Pseudo-scorpion

Glossary

Abdomen The rear part of an insect's body. It contains the insect's digestive system and sometimes ends in a stinger.

Ant A small insect that lives in a nest and gathers its food on plants or on the ground. Worker ants don't have wings, but they may have a stinger.

Antennae Two jointed organs on the head of an insect, which it uses for sensing things.

Aphid A small sap-sucking bug that lives on plants. Aphids are also known as greenfly or blackfly, depending on their color.

Bee A stinging insect that feeds at flowers. Some types of bee live in large nests, while others live on their own.

Beetle An insect that has thickened forewings, or elytra. When a beetle is on its feet, its elytra are closed up tightly.

Bug In everyday language, a bug is any kind of insect. To scientists, a "true bug" is a particular type of insect with piercing mouthparts and two pairs of wings. True bugs feed on plants and animals.

Butterfly An insect that has two pairs of wings covered in tiny scales and usually flies by day. Most butterflies feed at flowers.

Camouflage Colors or patterns that help an animal to hide by making it blend in with its background.

Centipede A long-bodied animal with one pair of legs on each of its body segments. Centipedes have a poisonous bite.

Cephalothorax In spiders, the front part of the body. The cephalothorax is usually much bigger than the head, and the spider's legs are attached to it.

Crab spider A spider that catches insects by lurking in flowers. Unlike most spiders, crab spiders are often brightly colored.

Crustacean An animal with a hard body, lots of pairs of legs, and two pairs of antennae. Apart from woodlice, most crustaceans live in the sea.

Damselfly An insect with a long, slender body and two pairs of transparent wings. Like dragonflies, damselflies grow up underwater.

Dragonfly A fast-flying insect with a long body and two pairs of stiff, transparent wings. Dragonflies grow up underwater.

Elytra Another word for a beetle's forewings. Elytra are much thicker than the beetle's hind wings, which they protect when the beetle is crawling around.

Entomologist Someone who studies insects.

Fangs In spiders, a pair of sharp mouthparts that stab into the spider's prey, injecting venom.

Feelers An everyday word for an insect's antennae.

Fly An insect that has only one pair of wings.

Forewings An insect's front wings. The forewings are often bigger than the hind wings, and in some insects they are thick or leathery.

Gall A plant growth used as a home by insects. The insects give off chemicals that make the galls grow.

Gall wasp Tiny wasps that grow up inside plant galls.

Grasshopper An insect with strong back legs and leathery forewings. Grasshoppers are very good at jumping and they feed on plants.

Grub A young beetle. Grubs look very different from adult beetles, and they often live inside their food.

Habitat The kind of surroundings that an animal normally lives in. Insect habitats include forests, deserts, and freshwater.

Hibernation A long winter sleep. Many insects hibernate, because they cannot move or find food when the weather gets cold.

Hind wings An insect's back wings.

Honeycomb A hanging sheet of wax full of small spaces, or cells. Honeybees make honeycombs to store honey and to raise their larvae.

Honeydew The sugary liquid that aphids produce when they feed.

Hoverfly A fast-flying insect that feeds on nectar. Hoverflies get their name because they often hover over flowers.

Jumping spider A spider that has large eyes and that catches its prey by jumping on to it instead of by making a web.

Lacewing A night-flying insect that has a slender body and two pairs of wings with lacy veins.

Larva (plural larvae) A young insect that looks very different from its parents and that changes shape as it grows up. Grubs, caterpillars, and maggots are all examples of larvae.

Leaf miner An insect grub that feeds by chewing or "mining" its way through the inside of a leaf.

Life cycle All the stages in an animal's life, from the moment it starts life to the moment when it has young.

Metamorphosis The change in shape that happens as an insect or other animal grows up.

Millipede A long-bodied animal with two pairs of legs on each of its body segments. Millipedes have hard bodies and often coil up into a spiral if they are touched.

Mimic A harmless animal that protects itself by looking like a dangerous one. Many insects use mimicry to survive.

Moth An insect that has two pairs of wings covered in tiny scales and usually flies by night. Most moths feed at flowers.

Nectar The sugary liquid that flowers make to attract insects.

Orb web A web with a circular shape.

Parasite An animal that feeds on the living body of another one.

Pedipalps (palps) Two small "arms" on either side of a spider's head. Spiders use their palps for signaling, mating, and for testing food.

Pollen The dustlike substance that plants produce.

Predator An animal that hunts others for food.

Pupa The stage in the life cycle of many insects, when the young insect's body is broken down and an adult one grows.

Queen bee In a bees' nest, the queen is the only bee that lays eggs. She controls the nest and is cared for by the worker bees. Wasps, ants, and termites also have queens.

Saddle In adult earthworms, a smooth band around the body, about one-third of the way down.

Scavenger Any animal that feeds on dead remains.

Solitary bee A bee that lives alone instead of living with other bees in a nest.

Termite A wood-eating insect that lives in a nest. Unlike ants, termites usually feed at night and they do not have stingers.

Thorax The middle part of an insect's body. The other two parts are the head and the abdomen.

Wasp A stinging insect with two pairs of wings, often colored yellow and black to show other animals that they are dangerous, so they leave them alone.

Worker An insect that lives in a nest and that carries out the daily tasks needed to keep the nest thriving. Unlike the queen, workers do not breed.

Index

Index: Hilary Bird

The publisher would like to thank the following for their kind permission to reproduce their photographs:

Key: a–above; c–center; b–below; l–left; r–right; t–top

Alamy Images: IPS 36tl; Robert Pickett/Papilio 21cr, 21ac; Simon de Trey-White/Photofusion Picture Library 66tl.
Ardea.com: John Daniels 66br; Pat Morris 67br; Steve Hopkin 32b.
Peter Chew - Brisbane Insects and Spiders: 29t.
Bruce Coleman Ltd: Andrew Purcell 62bl.
Corbis: 55tr; Angela Hampton; Ecoscene 8tr; George McCarthy 30–31b; Jim Sugar 67t; Ralph A. Clevenger 68–69; Robert Pickett 59tr; Wolfgang Kaehler 51t.

FLPA – images of nature: B. Borrell Casals 35cr.
Thomas R. Fletcher: 32–33c.
Holt Studios International: Nigel Cattlin 39bl.
N.H.P.A.: Ant Photo Library 53t; Anthony Bannister 13tr, 34–35b; Daniel Heuclin 22b; David Middleton 43b; Eric Soder 64bc; Ernie Janes 41br, 46–47; George Bernard 21cl, 35tl; Haroldo Palo Jr 42c; Mark Bowler 59cra; Martin Garwood 60br; N A Callow 57tr; N. A Callow 37cla; Peter Parks 58br; Robert Thompson 10br, 50cl; Stephen Dalton 11cl, 12–13, 45tr, 45crb, 48br, 65tr.
Nature Picture Library Ltd: Brian Lightfoot 36cr; Duncan McEwan 36bl, 39tr; Geoff Dore 16b, 25clb; Ingo Arndt 4b; John Downer 23t; Premaphotos 28cl, 55tl.
Premaphotos Wildlife: Ken Preston-Mafham 56cl.

Science Photo Library: Anthony Mercieca 51b; Barbara Strnadova 4–5; Claude Nuridsany & Marie Perennou 19t, 57b; Francoise Sauze 30cl; Jack K. Clark/Agstock 41tc; James H. Robinson 56tr; VVG 5br.
Warren Photographic: Kim Taylor 15cr, 17t 29cl, 31tr, 33tr, 34l, 44c, 46cl, 53bl, 54b.

All other images © Dorling Kindersley
www.dkimages.com